Headline Series

No. 292   **FOREIGN POLICY ASSOCIATION**   Spring 1990

UN Peacekeepers
Soldiers with a Difference
by Augustus Richard Norton
and
Thomas George Weiss

APPENDIX

Cover Design: Ed Bohon $4.00

The Authors

AUGUSTUS RICHARD NORTON is professor of political science at the United States Military Academy, West Point, New York. He served in 1980 and 1981 as an unarmed military observer attached to Unifil in southern Lebanon and in 1989 he was a Fulbright research professor in Norway where he worked on peacekeeping. Professor Norton has a Ph.D. from the University of Chicago and is currently at work on a book on culture and politics in the Middle East for Harcourt Brace Jovanovich. He would like to thank the United States Educational Foundation in Norway, the Norwegian Institute of International Affairs and the MacArthur Foundation for their support of his research.

THOMAS GEORGE WEISS is associate director at Brown University's Institute for International Studies. He served as executive director of the International Peace Academy (1985–89), after having been a permanent staff member of Unctad (1975–85). Dr. Weiss is a graduate of Harvard University and has two advanced degrees from Princeton University. He is the author of numerous articles and books on international politics, organization, conflicts and development.

The Foreign Policy Association

The Foreign Policy Association is a private, nonprofit, nonpartisan educational organization. Its purpose is to stimulate wider interest and more effective participation in, and greater understanding of, world affairs among American citizens. Among its activities is the continuous publication, dating from 1935, of the HEADLINE SERIES. The authors are responsible for factual accuracy and for the views expressed. FPA itself takes no position on issues of U.S. foreign policy.

HEADLINE SERIES (ISSN 0017-8780) is published four times a year, Winter, Spring, Summer and Fall, by the Foreign Policy Association, Inc., 729 Seventh Ave., New York, N.Y. 10019. Chairman, Michael H. Coles; President, John W. Kiermaier; Editor in Chief, Nancy L. Hoepli; Senior Editors, Ann R. Monjo and K.M. Rohan. Subscription rates, $15.00 for 4 issues; $25.00 for 8 issues; $30.00 for 12 issues. Single copy price $4.00. Discount 25% on 10 to 99 copies; 30% on 100 to 499; 35% on 500 to 999; 40% on 1,000 or more. Payment must accompany all orders. Add $1.75 for postage. USPS #238-340. Second-class postage paid at New York, N.Y. POSTMASTER: Send address changes to HEADLINE SERIES, Foreign Policy Association, 729 Seventh Ave., New York, N.Y. 10019. Copyright 1990 by Foreign Policy Association. Composed and printed at Science Press, Ephrata, Pennsylvania. Spring 1990.

Library of Congress Catalog Card No. 90-82248
ISBN 0-87124-133-1

Introduction

"Regional conflict may well threaten world peace as never before."

—President George Bush
UN General Assembly, September 25, 1989

A lfred Nobel hardly intended to honor soldiers when he created the peace prize that bears his name, and no military organization had received the prize throughout its 87-year history until December 1988 when United Nations peacekeepers—soldiers with a difference—were selected to join Henry Kissinger, George C. Marshall, Mother Teresa and Archbishop Desmond Tutu, among others, as recipients of the prestigious award. The setting for the presentation of the prize was the Oslo University Åula, where an Edvard Munch mural of a radiant sunrise is an apt symbol of the renaissance of UN peacekeeping in the past four years.

The Nobel Prize committee was reminding the world of the crucial contribution to conflict management made by UN peacekeepers, lightly armed soldiers who use force only in self-defense and as a last resort. The forces are symbolic neutral military units deployed between belligerents who have agreed to cease fighting. They are created by the UN Security Council, after the secretary-general has received the assent of the belligerents. Typically, the troops are drawn from countries outside of the region to which they are assigned.

Peacekeeping is tough and frustrating work. As Sir Brian Urquhart—the former UN under secretary for special political affairs, whose extended involvement in UN operations has earned him the informal title of "Mr. Peacekeeper"—wrote recently: "There have been times where the peacekeeping function was more like that of an attendant in a lunatic asylum, and the soldiers had to accept abuse and harassment without getting into physical conflict or emotional involvement with the inmates." In fact, in hazardous areas like southern Lebanon, UN peacekeepers have not only been harassed, but have been mugged, beaten, kidnapped and murdered in the course of conducting their duties. Although peacekeeping operations can be dangerous, UN soldiers are under orders to avoid force and turn the other cheek.

The UN Charter provides for the establishment of a standing military force, and a military oversight committee (see page 56 of Appendix for relevant UN Charter Articles), but no standing UN military force has ever been created, and the oversight committee has been ineffectual. In the absence of a permanent UN army, peacekeeping forces have been cobbled together by the secretary-general.

From the heights of Kashmir to the valleys of southern Lebanon and the deserts of Namibia, soldiers under the UN flag have helped keep the peace for the last four decades. They have verified facts, monitored cease-fires and reported on compliance with international agreements. They have helped overcome mistrust and end wars between nations and even within nations. They derive much of their influence from the moral weight of the international community: when they have its full support, these forces can make a difference.

In 1988 alone, three peacekeeping operations were launched, and in 1989 two more. (The chronology on pages 54 and 55 lists the 10 ongoing operations and the countries contributing military personnel to them.) The troops for these operations have been contributed by more than a quarter of the UN's 159-nation membership. The locales in which peacekeepers are deployed are frequently areas of strategic importance to the United States, as the map depicting the current peacekeeping operations shows (see page 8).

The five most recent operations illustrate peacekeeping's contributions to regional security. Unarmed UN observers were dispatched to Afghanistan in April 1988 to verify the withdrawal of the Soviet Army after the signing of the Geneva accords which followed several years of UN-brokered talks between the Kabul government and the Afghan rebels. On the Iraq-Iran border, the eight-year-old Persian Gulf war sputtered to a close in August 1988, after as many as a quarter of a million people had been slaughtered. The tenuous cease-fire was monitored by another group of observers. Still other UN observers monitored the departure from Angola of the Cuban combat troops that had provided support since 1975 to the Luanda government in its internal war against rebel leader Jonas Savimbi. They were assigned there under the December 1988 comprehensive security agreements in southern Africa.

The momentum continued in 1989. In April, after numerous false starts since 1978, a 7,000-man UN force of soldiers, police and civilians was deployed to Namibia to oversee that country's transition from South African rule to independence.

Peacekeepers in Central America

In November 1989, the Security Council unanimously approved a peacekeeping force as part of international efforts to stop strife in Central America. It was only the second time—the first was in 1965 in the Dominican Republic crisis—that the Security Council had approved a UN operation in the Western Hemisphere. Military observers are to verify that no more outside military aid is supplied to insurgents (notably Honduran-based Nicaraguan contras as well as rebels in El Salvador) and that no country's territory is used for attacks against another (especially Nicaragua). The movement toward peace in the area was punctuated dramatically in February 1990 by UN-supervised elections in which the revolutionary government of Nicaraguan

President Daniel Ortega Saavedra was voted out of office. As the Namibian operation wound down, armed UN forces were transferred to Nicaragua to collect the weapons of guerrillas. These essential tasks were key elements of the Central American peace process launched by the Contadora Group in 1983 and continued under the auspices of the five Central American presidents, most notably the former president of Costa Rica, Oscar Arias Sánchez.

A peacekeeping operation and a UN-administered plebiscite are on the drawing board for the Western Sahara, where Moroccan territorial claims are opposed by the Polisario liberation front, which claims that the former Spanish Sahara colony is entitled to independence.

In August 1989, on the eve of the Vietnamese withdrawal from Cambodia after 10 years of occupation, a contingency plan for a so-called International Control Mechanism awaited agreement between the government of Prime Minister Hun Sen and the three opposition parties led by Prince Norodom Sihanouk. Then, in January 1990, Australia proposed turning Cambodia over to a temporary UN administration with UN peacekeepers ensuring security. The plan was approved by the permanent members of the Security Council at a special meeting in Paris. The implementation of the preliminary agreement awaits extensive consultation and action by the full membership of the Security Council, not to mention the assent of the Cambodian belligerents.

The recent successes of UN peacekeepers have spawned proposals to assign them even more-ambitious tasks. These include interdicting the illicit international drug trade, countering terrorism and providing humanitarian services in areas stricken by man-made or natural disasters. Before assessing the suitability of UN forces for such missions, it is appropriate to consider peacekeeping's evolution, its strengths and its limitations.

Peacekeeping's Landscape

The UN was conceived by the United States and its allies in World War II. Even before hostilities ceased, 51 nations, all of whom were aligned against one or more of the Axis powers, signed the UN Charter in San Francisco on June 26, 1945. Reflecting their conviction that one of the causes of the war had been the lack of a collective-security mechanism, the UN Charter's principles include the renunciation of the threat or use of force and the peaceful settlement of disputes and, should that fail, a unified response to aggression. This last principle, designed to give the UN organization the capacity to enforce the peace, distinguished it from its predecessor, the League of Nations. And, in the brief interval between the end of World War II and the beginning of the cold war, it actually seemed as if a world order characterized by reason, law and collective security was feasible. However, the Soviet Union's establishment of a Communist bloc in Eastern Europe and the victory of the Communists in China in 1949 ended the big-power cooperation on which the postwar order was predicated. Under the UN Charter, collective decision-making required unanimity among the five permanent members

Where UN Forces Keep the Peace

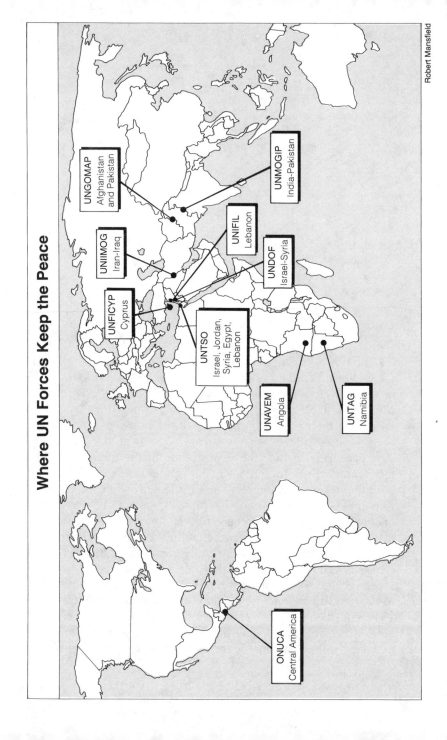

UNGOMAP
Afghanistan and Pakistan

UNMOGIP
India-Pakistan

UNIIMOG
Iran-Iraq

UNIFIL
Lebanon

UNDOF
Israel-Syria

UNFICYP
Cyprus

UNTSO
Israel, Jordan, Egypt, Syria, Lebanon

UNAVEM
Angola

UNTAG
Namibia

ONUCA
Central America

Robert Mansfield

of the Security Council—Britain, China, France, the Soviet Union and the United States—each of whom had a veto. With its members polarized into two camps, free world and Communist, the UN was unable to maintain the peace and prevent conflict.

The Birth of Peacekeeping

Peacekeeping is nowhere described in the UN Charter. It is often referred to in the words of UN Secretary General Dag Hammarskjöld (1953-61) as Chapter Six and a Half because it falls between Chapter VI of the Charter, which calls for the peaceful resolution of conflict, and Chapter VII on the use of enforcement measures should negotiation fail. The development of Chapter Six and a Half was the product of a sensible U.S. decision that international enforcement measures were impractical.

The UN assigned military personnel in 1947 to the Consular Commission on Indonesia and the Special Committee on the Balkans, but they were not under the direct authority of the secretary-general. The first soldiers dispatched under his authority were sent to the Middle East after the Arab-Israeli war of 1948-49 and the establishment of the state of Israel.

From these first military observers deployed in Palestine in 1948 to the establishment of the UN force in Lebanon in 1978, the United States was the champion of what became known as peacekeeping. Washington paid for at least 30 percent of the assessed and voluntary budgets for peacekeepers, and often much more. In addition, the United States routinely donated essential matériel and provided logistic support—the expensive airlifting of troops and equipment at the beginning of operations—at no cost to the UN.

Until the Gorbachev era, the Soviet Union and the United States did not see eye to eye on peacekeeping. The Soviet Union repeatedly tried to obtain a greater voice in UN decisions about peacekeeping and, when it failed, tried to defeat peacekeeping missions, but it was outmaneuvered by the United States and its supporters. The United States opposed a Soviet role in peacekeeping for fear of strengthening Moscow's influence in the Third

World. Even after decolonization changed the numerical balance in the UN in favor of the Soviet Union, Washington successfully limited Moscow's participation at the UN in regional diplomacy and regional conflicts.

To a large degree, Soviet opposition toward UN peacekeeping can be traced to the experience of the U.S.S.R. with three of the earliest and most extensive operations—the Korean War, the Suez Canal crisis and the civil war in the Belgian Congo. In all three cases, the Kremlin's foreign policy objectives were thwarted.

The Korean operation of 1950 was approved by the UN Security Council after North Korea, a Soviet ally, invaded South Korea. At the time the Soviet Union was boycotting the Security Council to protest China's continued representation by the defeated Nationalist government on Taiwan instead of by the People's Republic of China. After the Security Council vote, the Soviet Union hurriedly returned to its seat and objected to the operation. The General Assembly subsequently passed the Uniting for Peace Resolution, authorizing the Assembly to act when the Security Council was paralyzed, and the operation continued.

The UN involvement in Korea was largely symbolic, since the Security Council delegated command of the 16-nation force, the UN Unified Command in Korea, to the United States. The UN maintains that the Korean action was not "peacekeeping" but rather a "special case," both because there was not an international command structure and because force was used routinely, not only in self-defense. The United States claims that Korea was a peacekeeping operation, but its view is not widely shared. China, for example, before expressing a recent interest in peacekeeping, asked for assurance that Korea was an exception to standard peacekeeping procedures and that the primacy of the Security Council is the norm. China has sent military officers on a visiting mission to UN operations in the Middle East and now supports a UN peacekeeping role in Cambodia.

Following the British-French-Israeli invasion of the Suez Canal Zone in 1956, the Soviet Union proposed to the United States a joint response, but Washington refused because it did not want Soviet ground troops in the Middle East. Instead Washington favored—and Moscow opposed—a UN emergency force drawn from nonpermanent members of the Security Council. Once again the Uniting for Peace Resolution—which many international lawyers consider a doubtful legal tool—was used to create a neutral UN force, composed of units from 10 countries, among them Canada, Brazil, India, Norway and Sweden, which was stationed along the Suez Canal. This was the first time the term "peacekeeping force," coined by Canadian Prime Minister Lester Pearson, was used. The Soviet Union and France refused to pay their share. Moscow continued to withhold its payments for peacekeeping until 1973.

Peacekeeping Limitations

The experience in the Congo (now Zaïre), where UN forces became embroiled in a civil war, suggests lessons about the limits of peacekeeping. The 1960–64 UN Operation in the Congo (ONUC)* functioned under chaotic conditions, with a loosely drawn mandate and without a firm base of international support. This force was successful in preventing the dismemberment of the former Belgian colony, as well as in extricating foreign mercenaries; but both sides—the Soviet-backed government of Prime Minister Patrice Lumumba and the U.S.-supported president, Joseph Kasavubu—blamed ONUC for favoring the other. The fact that the operation ultimately served to remove a radical nationalist leader in favor of a more Western-oriented one turned many African leaders against peacekeeping until the recent Namibia operation. France and the Soviet Union again refused to pay their share of the cost, leaving the United States to pick up the lion's share. The UN had to float bonds to pay the bills. The Soviet Union could have lost its voting rights for failing to pay its Congo assessment, and this would have wrecked the UN.

In all three cases, Moscow objected particularly to the independent exercise of authority by the secretary-general and retaliated by becoming increasingly critical of UN peacekeeping and sour toward the possibility of new operations.

Abbreviations used in the text are written out in a list on page 64.

Peacekeeping in Intractable Conflicts

The peacekeeper's function is to separate belligerents, whether they be nations, warring tribes or militias fired by ideological or communal passions. The preferred, and certainly the least problematic, role for international peacekeepers is to separate the forces of nations that have agreed, at least, to avoid war. But not all peacekeeping operations are deployed where adversaries wish a cease-fire, or where the mission may be neatly described by so many lines on a map.

When peacekeepers are interposed between warring countries, they tend to deploy along borders, thereby creating areas of separation, or buffer zones. But when they are inserted in a civil or internal war, boundaries are by no means as easily drawn. So peacekeepers often are forced to police shifting internal lines in an effort to stop bloodshed. Whereas operations like the UN Disengagement Observer Force (Undof) on Syria's Golan Heights deploy as a result of meticulously negotiated agreements, peacekeeping in the context of internal warfare may not always be so carefully crafted. If international conflict is frequently difficult to resolve, internal strife is even more difficult to eradicate. An admixture of soldiers, often speaking neither the language of diplomacy nor of the local population, should not be expected to succeed where skilled mediators have failed.

For instance, the UN Interim Force in Lebanon (Unifil) was created in 1978 to oversee the withdrawal of Israeli forces and the reestablishment of Lebanese governmental authority in the southern part of the country. Yet it quickly found itself in the midst of an array of gunmen and militiamen, who, in the aggregate, represent nearly every active conflict in the Middle East. UN peacekeepers at present do provide a real measure of security to that part of Lebanon that is the UN's area of operation, but restoring the authority of the nonexistent central government and forcing the Israeli Defense Forces (IDF) to leave is well beyond the capacities of some 6,000 blue-helmeted peacekeepers.

Cyprus provides another example of a situation in which a UN force has been asked to do the impossible, namely to solve the formidable diplomatic puzzle of an old conflict between the Greek

United Nations/Photo by J. K. Isaac

Unifil soldier from Norway serving as observer to confirm the withdrawal of Israeli forces from southern Lebanon.

and Turkish Cypriots. From 1964 to 1974 the UN Force in Cyprus (Unficyp) was deployed throughout the island, where it functioned as a constabulary force and succeeded in quelling intercommunal bloodshed.

Its role changed dramatically when an Athens-sponsored coup in 1974 precipitated a Turkish invasion which, in turn, led to the division of the island into Greek and Turkish communities. Since 1974 the Cyprus force has served as a buffer separating the Turkish-occupied North from the southern part where the Greek Cypriot majority resides. In many ways, the operation became more like a successful interstate peacekeeping force after 1974. The belligerents agreed to a cease-fire and occupied a well-defined territory, while UN soldiers patrolled along the "green line" that demarcates the de facto division of the island and its capital, Nicosia. The secretary-general has continuously sought to keep the two parties at the bargaining table while the force has carried out its assignments. Critics of the Cyprus force argue that through its presence it has stabilized the division of Cyprus and impeded a resolution of the conflict, but they offer no satisfactory alternative. Cyprus remains a tinderbox on the southern flank of the Western defense alliance, the North Atlantic Treaty Organization (NATO), where Greece and Turkey could become embroiled once again in a head-on confrontation.

Toward a Consensus

It was not until the Middle East crisis of 1973 that the Soviet Union began to modify its hostility toward peacekeeping. On October 6, 1973, Egypt and Syria, generously equipped with Soviet arms, launched coordinated attacks to recapture territories occupied by Israel since the 1967 war. The first days of the war were marked by stunning Israeli reversals. On the Golan Heights, a massive Syrian armor assault nearly dislodged Israel's forces and was only repulsed with great difficulty. In the Sinai, the Egyptians seized two major footholds after demolishing an Israeli defense line, designed to be impregnable, along the Suez Canal. When the Israeli counterattack in the Sinai threatened to envelop the Egyptian attackers, the Soviet Union alerted airborne forces that could intervene in the fighting, and President Richard M. Nixon responded by calling a worldwide alert of U.S. military forces. Deft diplomatic moves by both superpowers, in support of UN Security Council-mandated cease-fires, defused the crisis.

After the October war, Secretary of State Kissinger and Soviet Foreign Minister Andrei Gromyko agreed that each of the superpowers would provide 36 military observers to the existing UN Truce Supervision Organization (Untso) to help monitor the cessation of hostilities. While the United States had been represented in Untso since 1948, Soviet participation was new and symbolically important. Moreover, the Soviets agreed to help finance UN forces in the Sinai and on the Golan Heights. The latter force (Undof) is a remarkable balance of soldiers from NATO, the Warsaw Pact (the Soviet-East European military alliance), and neutral countries interposed between the Israeli and Syrian armies. Since 1974, a Polish logistics battalion has supported the Austrians patrolling on the Syrian side of the Golan Heights, while a Canadian counterpart is deployed on the Israeli side in support of a Finnish contingent.

Between the Congo operation in the early 1960s and the October 1973 war when the Soviet attitude began to shift, attempts had been made to reconcile Washington's and Moscow's differing approaches to peacekeeping. The so-called Committee of 33—the UN Special Committee on Peacekeeping (which consists of 34 members since China's admission in 1988)—provided a forum for a dialogue between the superpowers. It led to the negotiation of Draft Formulae for Articles of Agreed Guidelines for UN Operations (see pages 60–63 of Appendix).

These principles were devised by the secretary-general and his staff to provide guidance for the Security Council, the secretary-general, host countries, force commanders, and other UN member states. The guidelines, for example, specify that the secretary-general establishes, directs and controls peacekeeping operations only under the authority of the Security Council. In composing peacekeeping forces, geographic balance is explicitly declared to be a "guiding principle." Another principle stresses that the financing of operations shall be borne by all members as required by the UN Charter. The still-evolving document has by no means closed all of the loopholes or met all of the objections of member states, but it represents a significant step in the right direction.

Although some political differences remain, the UN has followed these principles in practice since 1973, including the last five operations. In fact, the existence of these generally agreed principles probably influenced the recent major Soviet shift in attitude toward peacekeeping.

Decline and Revival, 1981–87

The U.S. attitude toward peacekeeping and the UN in general has also shifted dramatically over the last decade. When Ronald Reagan defeated Jimmy Carter for the presidency in 1980, one of his campaign themes was that the United States had become "soft" in the post-Vietnam War era and needed to roll back Soviet gains in the Third World. A decade of unchecked Soviet activism and adventurism had increased Moscow's clientèle and influence throughout the Third World. U.S. policy had to change. One of the main arenas for indicating that "America is back" was the

UN. In contrast to what it saw as the Carter Administration's timidity in responding to anti-U.S. tirades by Third World radicals, the new Administration was determined to speak out and rebut its critics.

If U.S. public support for the UN was weak before the Reagan presidency, it declined even further in the 1980s. Many Americans saw the world organization as little more than a forum for long-winded, tiresome debates and diatribes. The official U.S. attitude toward the UN was even less friendly as the Administration abandoned Washington's traditional support for multilateral approaches to regional security in favor of a series of unilateral actions, including military intervention in Grenada, the bombing of Libya and the financing of anti-Communist insurgents in Afghanistan, Cambodia, Nicaragua and Angola. Articles with titles like "The Twilight of Internationalism" became standard fare in the leading foreign policy journals.

The Reagan Administration's conservative constituency, including the Washington-based Heritage Foundation, a think tank, was particularly distrustful of the world body. In addition to withdrawing from the UN Educational, Scientific and Cultural Organization (Unesco) because of mismanagement and politicization, the Administration began to use its Security Council veto with unaccustomed regularity. The Administration was not alone in its hostility toward the UN. Congressional critics of the organization forced the United States to renege on its financial commitments by refusing to vote funds to pay assessed dues, including those for peacekeeping. This plunged the UN from 1985 to 1987 into a financial crisis so deep that it almost wrecked the world organization.

By withholding contributions, Congress sought to pressure the UN and the majority of its members, Third World countries who often blocked U.S.-supported initiatives, to change their ways. Specifically, the Congress insisted that the UN institute budgetary and managerial reforms and curb the practice of permitting the short-term assignment of officials to the Secretariat. (The first loyalty of an official on abbreviated service is likely to be to his or her government, not to the UN.)

After three decades of reprimanding the Soviet Union for its lack of cooperation and refusal to pay bills, the United States suddenly became responsible for much of the red ink in the UN's financial accounts. But it is not the only member state with large debts. South Africa (since its ejection from many UN bodies) and Iran (since the 1978–79 revolution) have also fallen significantly behind in payments for the regular budget, and the Soviet Union, promises notwithstanding, still owes some $125 million for special peacekeeping assessments. But the U.S. debt constitutes well over one half the money owed the UN, which is about $1 billion. These debts create cash-flow problems of immense proportions for the UN and raise serious doubts about the organization's ability to underwrite future peacekeeping ventures.

Soviet and U.S. Policy Shifts

While the Reagan Administration was spurning the UN, the U.S.S.R. was discovering its utility for containing regional crises. The Soviet army was bogged down in a protracted counterinsurgency in Afghanistan, and Soviet military assistance programs in Cuba, Vietnam, Afghanistan, Angola and elsewhere were draining the treasury. There was an urgent need to shift expenditures from the military to finance the domestic policy of *perestroika*, or restructuring. Moscow therefore began to heed those of its diplomats and scholars who believed the world organization could contribute to managing international conflict.

The signal that Soviet policy toward peacekeeping had changed came in 1986, when the Soviets announced they would pay their assessment for the UN forces in Lebanon. This decision startled UN watchers, because the Soviets had agreed to go along with the deployment of the force in Lebanon only on condition that they would not be expected to provide financial support. Even more surprising was the Soviet Union's 1987 decision to begin reimbursing—in hard currency—its regular budget and peacekeeping debts of over $200 million. Moreover, the Kremlin agreed to the UN-sponsored indirect talks on Afghanistan that led to the Geneva accords and UN participation in monitoring the withdrawal of Soviet combat troops, a helpful face-saving device.

Soviet behind-the-scenes cajoling of Cuba and Vietnam to reach negotiated settlements in Angola and Cambodia respectively lent additional credibility to the U.S.S.R.'s declared change in policy.

Initially, many officials in Washington dismissed the Soviet posture as grandstanding intended to embarrass the United States, especially over its withholding of assessments. But even cynics were soon forced to concede that the Kremlin might, in fact, be quite serious in its newfound support of the UN.

Revision of the Soviet doctrine toward Third World conflicts had actually begun during the brief tenures of General Secretaries Yuri V. Andropov (1982–84) and Konstantin U. Chernenko (1984–85), but the most significant changes occurred after Mikhail S. Gorbachev assumed office in March 1985. It was at the 27th party congress in February 1986 that Moscow first called for a "comprehensive system of international security." Over the last four years, comprehensive security has evolved from a sweeping and vague compilation of economic, military and environmental measures to a set of discrete and, for the most part, feasible proposals for the prevention and containment of regional conflicts through the utilization of "peacekeeping operations in all their aspects," as one Soviet spokesman put it.

In his December 1988 address before the UN General Assembly, in which he made the dramatic announcement of unilateral arms reductions in Europe, Gorbachev devoted nearly three quarters of his time to endorsing the work of international organizations and outlining specific measures for using the UN in settling the conflict in Afghanistan. The specificity of his proposals gave credence to Moscow's stated support for making UN peacekeeping more solvent, active and effective. A principal architect of the new initiatives was Deputy Minister of Foreign Affairs Vladimir F. Petrovsky, a UN veteran and skilled technician in multilateral affairs.

The shift in Soviet attitudes evoked selective and positive responses from the United States, including crucial behind-the-scenes cooperation on particular regional conflicts. Consequently, the UN began to show a new vitality.

In his final speech to the General Assembly in September 1988,

President Reagan noted that "the UN has the opportunity to live and breathe and work as never before." In a remarkable about-face, Reagan complimented the secretary-general and the organization, and he specifically praised the utility of good offices and peacekeeping. Before leaving office, the President promised that the United States would pay its debts.

President Bush, himself a former ambassador to the UN, gave only cautious support to the organization in his first keynote address to the General Assembly in September 1989. But when he met with UN Secretary General Javier Pérez de Cuéllar, one of his first official dinner guests at the White House, the President received him warmly and promised him his full support. He appointed a skilled and seasoned diplomat, Thomas Pickering, to represent the United States at the UN. In an interview soon after he was appointed ambassador, Pickering stated that foremost among Washington's priorities was the desire to make better use of the UN's peacekeeping and peacemaking machinery in Third World conflicts.

Big-Power Cooperation

In November 1989 the Bush Administration joined the Soviet Union and all other members of the Security Council in authorizing unarmed UN military observers to depoliticize the conflict in Central America. Agreeing to admit UN peacekeepers into its sphere of influence was a major concession on the part of the United States. The two superpowers also broke precedent by cosponsoring a General Assembly resolution "to reinforce the work of the organization." The General Assembly adopted the resolution by consensus. As if to make certain that no one missed the new harmony in their relations, the heads of the Soviet and U.S. delegations held a joint press conference to publicize their bilateral stance. Notwithstanding some wrangling over a possible upgrading in the status of the Palestine Liberation Organization (PLO) at the UN that prompted Washington to threaten cutting off funding in December 1989, the United States clearly had come a long way toward restoring the reputation it enjoyed for most of the postwar era as the champion of multilateral cooperation.

The superpowers arrived at their reassessments of the UN's role in resolving or at least tempering stubborn regional conflicts through their own bitter experiences—the United States in Vietnam and the Soviet Union in Afghanistan. Both have paid high costs for their forays into the Third World, where force has proven to be of limited utility in settling disputes. Even the benefits of maintaining overseas bases and arming far-flung clients are no longer as clear as they once seemed. U.S.-Soviet rivalry in the Third World had hurt the superpower relationship and created "wars by proxy."

The dramatic improvement of relations between Moscow and Washington has enabled the Security Council since mid-1987 to function more or less as the collegial body anticipated in the UN Charter rather than as a great-power battleground. Today even cynical diplomats are speculating about the potential applications of the collective-security provisions described in Chapter VII of the UN Charter but rarely exercised, with the exception of the sanctions or other actions imposed against Rhodesia—now Zimbabwe—and the Republic of South Africa. This new mood of cooperation within the Security Council may enable the UN to forestall threats to international order in ways that seemed unthinkable only a few years ago.

2

Steps to Improve Peacekeeping

Enhanced superpower cooperation makes this a propitious time for the Bush Administration not only to utilize the UN's conflict-management mechanisms but also to explore how the UN may help meet other global challenges like terrorism, natural disasters, and the plague of illicit drugs. Admittedly, the prognosis for perestroika and *glasnost* (openness) is uncertain. It is no doubt unwise to pursue bilateral deals with the Soviet Union that are premised on Gorbachev's succeeding in his quest to reform the Soviet system and reshape his country's relations with the United States. But the appeal of working cooperatively with the Soviet Union to improve the capacity of the UN to prevent or at least contain regional conflict is that the benefits are likely to persist regardless of the outcome of Gorbachev's efforts. In this sense, improving the peacekeeping regime is a risk-free venture for the United States. Should the dialogue between Moscow and Washington come to an end, the United States, with its veto power in the Security Council, retains the capacity to block any UN operation that threatens its security interests.

International support for UN peacekeeping, symbolized by the

Nobel Peace Prize of 1988, appears at an all-time high. In addition to its recent successes in helping to create the preconditions for settlements in Afghanistan, the Persian Gulf, Angola, Namibia and Central America, the UN stands poised to play a leading part in ending the 20-year civil war in Cambodia, and plans are already under way for a plebiscite in the Western Sahara. Even the Cyprus dispute, which has dogged the UN for a quarter of a century, may yet be resolved despite the present stalemate.

Partly as a result of U.S. pressure, the organization has instituted budgetary reforms and lately managed to mitigate bloc politics, particularly the North-South and East-West confrontations that marred its earlier years. However, it is time for Washington to take new policy initiatives at the UN. U.S. policymakers should focus on two types of issues: policies necessary to improve traditional peacekeeping operations in the immediate future, and institutional innovations that would enable the UN to expand its operations to meet new challenges in the 1990s.

The traditional model of peacekeeping has worked well when parties to a conflict allow the interposition of neutral forces under international control. But unless the United States cooperates in urgently addressing three unresolved peacekeeping problems— financing, management and peacemaking—the current euphoria surrounding the UN as a critical element in the quest for international peace and security could turn quickly into disenchantment.

Paying the Bill

Any discussion of peacekeeping's future viability must begin with the thorny issue of financing. Since the start-up costs of all new operations and the burden of large undertakings, like the operation in Namibia, are funded directly from the regular UN budget, the organization's overall financial health is critical. While fiscal disaster was averted in 1985–87, acute financial difficulties persist. At the beginning of 1990, the United States, which, as the world's wealthiest nation, is assessed at the highest rate for both the regular budget and peacekeeping, still owed over $600 million. (The UN's 1990 regular budget is $987.3 million, of which the U.S. share is 25 percent.)

The five new operations that were authorized between April 1988 and the end of 1989, when combined with existing ones, increased the peacekeeping budget from a little over $200 million in 1987 to over $800 million in 1989. At the beginning of 1990, an interim UN administration and peacekeeping operation for Cambodia was agreed to in principle, an operation that could easily cost over $1 billion. A smaller operation for the Western Sahara was in the detailed planning stage. While the operation in Namibia has wound down, the work of the observer group in Central America has expanded. The annual peacekeeping budget could easily reach between $1.5 billion and $2 billion annually. Without increased revenues, there are serious doubts about the organization's ability to manage its cash-flow problems or, ultimately, to deploy and operate an array of armed military forces and unarmed military observers.

Moscow is apparently willing to consider new financing strategies. It has virtually eliminated its regular budget arrears and has made progress in reducing the level of its peacekeeping debts, although some of the payments in nonconvertible rubles still pose problems. The Soviet Union, having become a leading proponent of fiscal responsibility, may be receptive if the United States moves to reopen the debate about diversifying the sources of financing. Because member states will not be willing to contribute to peacekeeping operations on the same basis as they have in the past, consideration should be given to a variety of new measures.

Taxes on the beneficiaries should be considered, not only the host countries but also private companies whose balance sheets are more profitable as a result of successful conflict management. Since the end of hostilities in the Persian Gulf, for example, shipowners' savings from reduced insurance premiums alone could well have paid for the observer presence on the Iran-Iraq border as well as an endowment to fund other operations in the region. A procedure for collecting user fees of this sort was established when the Suez Canal was cleared following the 1973

Arab-Israeli war. The surtax was collected by the Suez Canal Company and then remitted to the UN treasury. A peace tax of as little as one cent for every barrel of oil put on board a tanker in the Persian Gulf could yield more than $50 million yearly.

Other measures must be examined. For instance, soliciting donations from the public and raising funds on the commercial markets should be considered, as nongovernmental organizations and even UN bodies like the UN Children's Fund (Unicef) and the World Bank do presently. Serious thought should also be given to the possibility of member states placing contingents at the disposal of the UN without reimbursement. Such a measure would reverse current practice but revive the operating procedure originally envisaged for UN military forces. But as long as the great powers are not paying their share of the peacekeeping budget, proposals of this type will be unpalatable.

A first step would be for the United States to pay its outstanding assessments. Moreover, the United States should not wait until the last moment to pay current bills. This has become standard practice because it allows Congress and the executive branch to exert maximum leverage over the UN. Furthermore, when an operation is approved, the United States should lead the way in meeting immediately its international obligations.

Beyond this, the Bush Administration should recognize that peacekeeping is a cost-effective mechanism for stabilizing areas of geostrategic and political importance. The U.S. share of the Namibia operation is approximately $128 million, about one quarter of the total budget for the force. This is the equivalent of 4 percent or less of the annual U.S. budget for the elite 82d Airborne Division. An influential military analyst of the U.S. defense budget conservatively estimates the direct and indirect annual budget for a first-line U.S. army division at between $3 billion and $4 billion. These costs help put in perspective UN peacekeeping bills, even substantially increased ones, that are shared by all member states.

As the Security Council's debates about Namibia demonstrated, the major powers take a niggardly approach to funding peacekeeping operations. The five permanent members quibbled

Untag military policemen from Kenya, part of a 7,000-man UN force, arriving in Windhoek in 1989 to help implement the independence plan for Namibia.

UN Photo by M. Grant

about finances and ignored the concerns of African and non-aligned states, and they mandated drastic reductions in the complement of the UN Transition Assistance Group (Untag). In cutting costs, the five indicated clearly that the financial tail is still wagging the dog: the operation was tailored to the financial authorization rather than having the tasks determine the appropriate composition of the force. The first few embarrassing days of the UN-controlled independence process ironically witnessed the highest casualties in the 23 years of guerrilla struggle. This shaky beginning not only jeopardized the future of Namibia's independence but called into question the ability of the UN to play an effective role in Africa.

Questions are increasingly asked about the willingness of the global community to finance an annual peacekeeping budget approaching $2 billion. Yet the more apt question pertains to the cost of alternatives, not only in financial terms but in terms of threats to regional and international stability—not to mention tragic human costs in suffering and forgone development. In the past, Washington and Moscow paid dearly for their competition for influence in the Third World. By any estimate, these costs dwarf those of peacekeeping.

The United States and the Soviet Union, as the two leading

contributors to peacekeeping operations, should encourage the other main contributors (Japan, France, the Federal Republic of Germany and Britain) to help meet future funding needs. The simple practice of paying assessments on time would help alleviate some of the UN's financial problems. No penalty has ever been levied for late payment of assessed dues, despite the fact that the Charter (Article 19) specifies that member states two years in arrears will lose their right to vote in the General Assembly. (The failure to invoke this rule against the Soviet Union and France after the Congo crisis is viewed as a precedent.) Both large and small states are delinquent. In the case of peacekeeping budgets, eight countries account for almost 85 percent of the total owed; the United States and the Soviet Union alone account for almost 45 percent. If the organization is to cope with the financial burden, the superpowers must set the example.

Countries that have traditionally supplied troops use their own cost-benefit calculations. Their support for peacekeeping has not only reflected hardheaded calculations about national defense policy but also about Western interests and values. While more than 40 countries have personnel among the 15,000 peacekeepers presently in UN service, the bulk of the burden is carried by the Nordic countries (Finland, Norway, Sweden, Denmark), Austria, Ireland and Canada. These countries consider peacekeeping an integral part of their foreign policies. Some also view such service as useful training for their soldiers. In addition, in the view of NATO allies like Norway and Canada, providing troops to a UN force is a form of burden-sharing and probably deserves to be recognized as such. By the same token, the contribution of peacekeepers in Third World conflicts could be considered as foreign aid for development. Given the importance of conflict management in establishing preconditions for investments in economic and social development, peacekeeping and troop contributions should be included as part of a government's official development assistance.

After financing, the second most serious problem confronting peacekeeping is overall management. An internal reorganization in 1988 sought to strengthen the UN secretary-general's role in negotiations and to centralize the conduct of ongoing peacekeeping operations and the planning of future ones in the Office of Special Political Affairs. However, this created a somewhat artificial division between peacemaking and peacekeeping, which may impede the success of future operations.

Administrative and Logistical Backup

Despite some improvements in the last couple of years, the UN is still unable to provide adequate administrative and logistical support for its military forces and observers in the field. Until 1987, the chief administrative officers attached to each peacekeeping force in the field arguably had more leverage on some decisions than the force commanders under whom they served. Even though the ultimate authority of the force commanders has since been explicitly elaborated, there are still two parallel decisionmaking channels. Thus, key operational decisions often are subordinated to other considerations.

Although providing logistical and administrative support to peacekeepers may, at first glance, seem relatively simple, such decisions can have a profound effect on the operational effectiveness of a force and its ability to function smoothly in a tough political environment. There have been some remarkable blunders made in the name of administrative efficiency or logistical simplicity. For instance, in 1978 the UN force in Lebanon was assigned to oversee the withdrawal of Israeli forces from southern Lebanon. Yet many of its key facilities were located in Israel, thereby making it susceptible to Israeli pressure. As late as the mid-1980s, Israeli construction firms were still doing a lot of the work at the force's headquarters at Naquora, Lebanon. Thus, the Lebanon force facilitated the introduction of even more Israelis into Lebanon.

Among the unsolved and serious problems are the inadequacy of the support provided for field operations and the ineffectiveness of military advice. Experienced and knowledgeable personnel, both civilian and military, are in short supply within the UN Secretariat to cover even ongoing operations. If the present demand for peacekeeping continues and the anticipated expansion occurs, there will simply be insufficient qualified people to manage and direct the forces.

The founding generation of peacekeepers retired in the mid-1980s. Even before that, there were only a few dozen UN civilians with peacekeeping experience among the 10,000 UN employees in New York City. The hiring freeze imposed in the 1980s as part of overall financial cutbacks added to the shortage of qualified people. At a time of increased demand for peacekeeping, the UN's management capacity is stretched very thin. The quality of UN operations will suffer without an increase in the number of first-rate international civil servants in New York who also staff field operations on temporary assignment.

These are serious shortcomings that could make UN peacekeeping the victim of its own success—and of the dramatically improved international climate. The secretary-general is aware that the UN is in danger of being overwhelmed by demands for the services it uniquely can provide; however, he may not be able to resist the pressure from member states to create operations which might undermine the world organization.

Uneven professional military leadership has been a major weakness at headquarters and in the field. Peacekeeping is no place for generals with little command or field experience. It is no surprise that many governments are reluctant to release their best officers and diplomats for extended UN service, but peacekeeping in the 1990s will require people of talent and ingenuity. The secretary-general should have a list of resourceful and talented generals and staff officers who can pass muster and will be released promptly by their governments when the UN needs them. The necessity of assuring geographic balance in personnel selections is a fact of life at the UN, and the need for neutral senior officers often disqualifies excellent candidates. But regardless of the difficulties, it is the secretary-general's duty to put the best people in the job. At a minimum, the secretary-general should insist on multiple nominations for all important posts. In this way he will not be forced to make do with senior peacekeepers whose only qualification is that they are from a country which is acceptable in a given part of the world.

The secretary-general and his staff should be prepared to respond creatively when a crisis suddenly explodes. In the case of a Lebanon or an Afghanistan, the international community has to respond to fast-breaking events. Improvisation in an emergency is unavoidable and has some virtues, but there is no substitute for careful and detailed contingency planning of peacekeeping operations. All too typically, forces have been deployed with inadequate instructions and unclear orders, as well as without essential logistical support. According to a number of senior officials who have served in UN peacekeeping operations, New York officials tend to avoid making tough, potentially controversial decisions.

Advance Planning

Geography, mission, timing and force size, as well as political and economic considerations, will obviously vary from one peacekeeping operation to another. Since the spectacular failure of the Maginot Line, military establishments have been counseled to avoid preparing for the last war. Similarly, an important guideline for UN military operations should be to avoid preparing for the last conflict. There are no universal textbook solutions, but this does not obviate the need for meticulous planning, often long in advance of actual deployment, except in unexpected crises. In addition to the secretary-general's Office of Research and Collection of Information (ORCI) with some 20 officials, there is a recently established Peacekeeping Board. Although the former is not structured for contingency planning, it could be reorganized into a UN policy planning staff.

All professional military establishments operate staff colleges of one variety or another to train officers to conduct operations and do logistical and administrative planning. Procedures and techniques vary but the universal expectation is that staff officers will learn to prepare practical and analytically sound plans for transporting soldiers into their areas of operations, and to ensure that they can operate effectively once they get there.

It is a striking deficiency of the UN that there is no military planning unit. The secretary-general is forced to depend on whatever military advice he can glean from supportive governments as well as from his single military adviser. Most armies maintain a "war room" 24 hours a day to monitor field operations and to respond quickly when problems develop. With forces and observers deployed in the Middle East, Latin America, Asia and Africa, it would be appropriate for the UN to operate a "peace room," manned around-the-clock by military officers whose task would be to monitor developments, brief the secretary-general and his deputies and provide military advice when requested. No such facility now exists, with the result that urgent operational problems sometimes are only addressed after the fact.

This deficiency in the planning and management of peacekeeping operations must be addressed if some of the problems that have plagued previous peacekeeping operations are to be avoided in the future. The Soviet Union has suggested the revival of the Military Staff Committee (MSC) as a way of coming to grips with this problem—a proposal that has met with little enthusiasm. The UN Charter specifies that the MSC act as a military directorate when the Security Council decides on collective security or enforcement actions under Chapter VII of the Charter. The committee is composed of the five permanent members of the Security Council. Unable to agree on anything, it has been essentially moribund since 1947. Troop contributors are not keen to strengthen an organ that excludes them. However, if membership were expanded informally (i.e., without revising the Charter) to include troop-contributing countries, the committee could be a useful sounding board. Even now, nothing prevents the MSC from rendering advice on logistical matters when the secretary-general so requests, thereby increasing his access to expertise and knowledge.

A better solution may be for the secretary-general to request troop-contributing nations to donate qualified staff officers who would serve in New York on temporary assignment for periods of two to three years, for nonrenewable terms, as members of a Secretariat military staff. Most, if not all, governments with soldiers deployed in the field under the UN flag would welcome the opportunity to improve the quality of military advice available to the secretary-general. After all, it is their citizens who are on the UN front lines, where over 700 peacekeepers have been killed in the past 40 years. These officers would have the additional advantage of being able to speak knowledgeably with peacekeepers in the field and officials in capitals. At present, almost all communications must be addressed to one overworked and peripatetic under secretary. In fact, several troop contributors have offered to attach officers to the UN to assist in planning and supervising peacekeeping operations, but their offers have been spurned because of problems associated with quotas and geographic balance.

The idea is not to create yet another bureaucratic appendage in New York. The size of the staff should be nine or ten officers, all staff-college graduates with experience in doing precisely the sort of nuts-and-bolts planning they would be charged to perform for the UN. A dividend for the world community would be that a small number of competent military officers would return to their home countries with a fuller appreciation of the nuances, difficulties and potentials of peacekeeping operations. No doubt, some of these officers would later find themselves actually deployed with a peacekeeping force, where their experience would enhance their value and effectiveness.

Combining Peacekeeping and Peacemaking

The third and final problem with traditional peacekeeping has been the intractability of the warring parties and the inherent difficulty of the situations in areas such as the Middle East, Cyprus and Iran-Iraq. Although the dispatch of UN forces or observers may dampen violence, it does not signal the end of a conflict but rather the beginning of an opportunity to resolve it. International peacekeeping is an interim step—a stopgap—to buy time for active diplomacy. The breathing space purchased by peacekeepers is often essential to allow passions to cool and enmities to abate. The deployment of a lightly armed peacekeeping force is the equivalent of a global declaration of danger. To reiterate, such forces derive much of their influence from the moral weight of the international community. They emphasize the inherent menace of a particular situation and the momentary intention of the international community to pull out all of the diplomatic stops.

The dissipation of tension all too often coincides with the abatement of international interest. Once established, peacekeeping operations often take on lives of their own. As Herbert Nicholas, an Oxford don who wrote with great authority about the UN, noted a quarter of a century ago, there is a tendency for the fireman to turn into a lodger. A temporary stopgap thus ends up being confused with a solution and internal conflicts fester. Troop-contributing countries in particular have often come to regret that a temporary calm almost always slows or destroys the momentum for concerted diplomacy. Some of them have withdrawn from UN forces to demonstrate their impatience—e.g., the Swedes from Cyprus and the Dutch from Lebanon.

After the peacekeeping crisis in the mid-1960s, when the Congo operation almost bankrupted the UN, the Special Committee on Peacekeeping recommended that peacemaking and peacekeeping be linked. Subsequently the Security Council has followed the practice of proposing or authorizing the secretary-general to appoint a special representative who pursues diplomacy while peacekeepers do their job. While the linkage does not guarantee success—as Cyprus, where UN soldiers have served for over a quarter century, demonstrates—the most successful UN peacekeeping operations have gone hand in hand with mediation. For instance, the Syrian-Israeli clashes that followed the October 1973 war ended when Kissinger successfully engineered a disengagement agreement between the two parties. Stationing a UN buffer force on the Golan Heights made it possible to implement the carefully wrought agreement, although it has also halted any effort to negotiate a peace treaty between Israel and Syria.

The most successful *non*-UN peacekeeping forces have also exemplified the importance of using peacekeepers and peacemakers in tandem. Both the Multinational Force and Observers (MFO), created in conjunction with the 1979 Camp David agreements that ended the war between Egypt and Israel, and the Commonwealth Monitoring Force (CMF), established to monitor the implementation of the Lancaster House Agreements in

Rhodesia in 1980, were deployed after comprehensive accords had been signed. The MFO was deployed under Western auspices when the Soviet Union objected to having a UN force monitor a U.S.-brokered treaty. In today's more-favorable diplomatic climate, the MFO would almost certainly be under UN control, as it was originally envisaged in the Egyptian-Israeli treaty. In Rhodesia, Britain, as the former colonial authority, played a central role in actually bringing the government of Ian Smith and the opposition led by Robert Mugabe and Joshua Nkomo to the negotiating table. It was predictable that the peacekeeping force would be a largely British show, with four other Commonwealth countries playing modest supporting roles.

Diplomacy and Mediation

Despite their rather different histories, the multinational and Commonwealth forces were successes. Each illustrated the indispensable role that a peacekeeping force may play in conjunction with creative diplomacy. In general, when peacekeepers are used to verify the implementation of a carefully constructed agreement, they are maintaining a status quo that adversaries have agreed to accept, rather than buttressing a stalemate that one or more of the parties to the conflict will seek to upset.

Mediation is one area in which the superpowers have recently demonstrated that they can make a difference. Both the United States and the Soviet Union were important in the negotiations in southern Africa that ended in the December 1988 agreements linking the withdrawal of foreign troops (both Cuban and South African) from Angola and the beginning of the UN-sponsored independence process in Namibia. The superpowers can help convince their respective allies of the utility of disengagement and peaceful settlement. The compromises made by Cuba and Angola, on the one hand, and the Republic of South Africa, on the other, would hardly have been possible without significant arm-twisting by Washington and Moscow.

Particularly where they are primary arms suppliers to the belligerents, as in the Middle East, the superpowers have significant diplomatic leverage. In fact, an underexploited role for peacekeepers is to isolate the contagion of internal conflict while the superpowers work to circumscribe or even prevent the involvement of other powers who promote and sustain fighting. By keeping a lid on a volatile situation, peacekeepers give antagonists the time and opportunity to reconcile their differences.

Regional Organizations' Record

Regional organizations have not generally been successful in peacekeeping and are unlikely to be so in the near future. The abortive operations of the Arab League in Lebanon in 1976 and 1989 and of the Organization of African Unity (OAU) in Chad are cases in point. In Chad, for example, the OAU force began operations in late 1981, but lacked professional military expertise and requisite financing. But peacemaking by regional organizations can be effective if it is properly backed by major powers and the UN. While regional actors may be weak institutionally, they can often exert considerable diplomatic pressure on parties in conflict from the same region, especially when these regional diplomatic efforts enjoy the active support and blessing of the superpowers.

For example, the Association of Southeast Asian Nations (Asean), together with the United States and China, was instrumental in pressing the Soviet Union to reduce its backing for Vietnam's military presence in Cambodia. The change in Soviet policy was influential in speeding the process leading to the Vietnamese withdrawal in September 1989 and encouraging the parties in the conflict to begin to negotiate. Great-power solidarity (Soviet, American, British and French) subsequently led to China's decision in January 1990 finally to support a UN interim administration and peacekeeping force in Cambodia. Lasting peace in Central America could be similarly facilitated by unequivocal superpower support for mediation by Nicaragua's regional partners. The same could be said for OAU efforts in the Western Sahara.

In all of these undertakings, UN peacekeepers will no doubt be involved. However, their success will depend on the help they receive from active regional diplomacy. Thus, a crucial aspect of each operation should be a plan for engaging regional organizations, whether informally or formally, prior to, not after a peacekeeping force is put in the field.

The real puzzle is how to deploy effectively a peacekeeping force without at the same time undermining the sense of diplomatic urgency that inspired the creation of the force. A possible parliamentary tactic to facilitate diplomatic engagement might be to make "sunset" provisions by the Security Council part of any mandate for a peacekeeping operation. Specifying the termination date for a particular operation—say three years from the date of formation—would not be an irrevocable step. Instead, such a provision would simply make it more difficult to extend an operation. The sunset clause might specify a series of diplomatic objectives or goals to be reached by certain dates, thereby providing benchmarks against which diplomatic progress might be assessed. In contrast, the mandates for operations are currently renewed almost automatically every six months, and even an operation like the UN force in Lebanon is rarely subject to serious scrutiny in the Security Council. The sunset provision would provide the opportunity to exert pressure on the parties and on troop contributors.

In the present system there are some extraordinary anomalies. In spite of well-known problems, long-standing peacekeeping operations are continued because of the indispensable role they play in maintaining order, yet they run on IOUs. Reimbursements, and partial reimbursements at that, to troop contributors may run as far behind as eight years. If a given operation is essential, then the secretary-general should not have to go begging to see that it continues. Thus, another component of a sunset clause should be adequate funding. Approval for the continuation of an operation beyond a specified date should, nearly always, be contingent on satisfactory arrangements to pay the bill. In some cases, the belligerents in a conflict may be able to pay a portion themselves, and regional organizations like the OAU and the Organization of American States (OAS) should certainly help raise funds.

The Use of Force

Florence Nightingale once observed before the Royal Commission on the Crimean War that "whatever else hospitals do, they shouldn't spread disease." By the same token, peacekeeping forces, typically inserted into violent or potentially violent situations, must avoid adding to the mayhem. Peacekeepers can separate warring enemies, observe cease-fires and report violations, but they use force only as a last resort and in self-defense. Soldiers as peacekeepers must walk a very fine line. Not only must they operate with impeccable neutrality and exemplify military professionalism, but they must demonstrate restraint and self-control.

Peacekeeping forces seldom number more than 5,000 or 6,000 soldiers, and their armaments are lightweight, especially in comparison with the implements of modern warfare often available even to irregular forces. Moreover, the tasks assigned to peacekeepers may require them to be deployed over large areas, often in outposts or checkpoints manned by fewer than half a dozen soldiers. In addition, there are the extra problems inherent in coordinating the actions of units not just from different countries but from different cultures. Equipment, training, organization, language and experience vary tremendously from one contingent to another. Thus, if a UN peacekeeping force should find itself enmeshed in a shooting war, there is a good prospect that it would quickly be outgunned and outmaneuvered.

In conventional combat situations, aggressive tactics designed to crush the enemy are often a key to success; in peacekeeping the same tactics open the door to failure. Peacekeepers who put aside restraint may quickly find themselves part of the problem rather than part of the solution.

The cost of using force too zealously is illustrated by the experience of the Multinational Force in Beirut (MNF). Both Israel and Lebanon wanted an American presence on the ground. The MNF was designed as a non-UN force, composed of U.S., French, Italian and, later, British forces. It was deployed in the summer of 1982, after the Israelis laid siege to Beirut and called for a withdrawal of Syrian soldiers and Palestinian guerrillas. Initially, the force's duration was to be 30 days—just long enough to oversee the withdrawal of Palestinian combatants from Lebanon. It fulfilled this mission very competently. But within days of the withdrawal, in September 1982, President-elect Bashir Gemayel was assassinated and Israeli-supported Lebanese Maronite militiamen massacred hundreds of civilians in the Sabra and Chatila Palestinian refugee camps.

The multinational force was hastily recalled. MNF II (as it was called) succeeded, for a while, in instilling a measure of stability, but diplomacy could not keep pace with the deteriorating situation. The obduracy of the new government of President Amin Gemayel, who proved more intent on preserving the privileges of the established order than meeting legitimate demands for reform, angered Lebanese opponents, especially among the Shiite Muslims. Israel, having expunged Syrian and PLO forces from Beirut, felt little pressure to withdraw its forces and only reluctantly made room for the Western troops. Later, the Israeli forces would be mercilessly pummeled by Lebanese resistance factions and would be forced to retreat from the environs of Beirut and then from nearly all of Lebanon. Simultaneously, Syria and Iran, acting singly and together, conspired to reverse the outcome of the Israeli invasion by bolstering anti-regime forces and sponsoring a series of attacks upon the multinational force.

U.S. diplomats failed to take advantage of the respite that the multinational force purchased. Only after months of intense but hapless discussions did Washington's diplomats find their bearings in Lebanon. By then, the summer of 1983, the force's initial success had unraveled. The U.S. embassy had been demolished by a car bomb in April, moderate opposition forces had been defeated, and the Israeli occupation forces were under steady attack. By September 1983, the U.S. contingents in the multinational force had joined the fighting in Lebanon by providing artillery and airpower in support of the Lebanese army, an army that a sizable segment of the Lebanese took as their enemy. It is noteworthy that the decision to broaden the U.S. forces' mandate was made by the National Security Council staff over the strenuous objections of U.S. military commanders in the multinational force in Beirut and in disregard of the necessity of preventing the force from becoming embroiled in the conflict.

By becoming a participant in the conflict, the multinational force sacrificed its impartiality and moral authority and came to be viewed by opponents of the Gemayel government as simply another militia. In the vernacular, the force was now called the "international militia." The French and U.S. contingents were the target of horrendous suicide bombings that resulted in some 350 deaths in the autumn of 1983. The force withdrew in early 1984, leaving behind a country engulfed by war.

This case illustrates that it can be disastrous to ask peacekeepers to do what diplomacy has not done. The failure of the multinational force was by no means preordained. The force did buy time for diplomacy, but when that time was not well spent the force paid a dear price. Naval gunfire and artillery barrages serve as a poor substitute for effective peacemaking, especially in battle-hardened terrain like Lebanon. The lessons of past operations underline the wisdom of strictly constrained rules of engagement, as well as a carefully considered evaluation of how the use of force will buttress, or undermine, the purposes for which peacekeepers have been dispatched.

The nonuse of force can also be a disabling credo if it is interpreted to preclude resolve and resourcefulness. Since 1973 UN rules governing the use of force have been broadened from "individual" to "institutional" self-defense. In plain language this means that peacekeepers are permitted to use force not only in personal self-defense but also to resist all attempts aimed at preventing a UN operation from carrying out essential parts of its mandate.

Casualties are part of peacekeeping. The governments of contributing nations are understandably deeply concerned when their soldiers die in UN service. The practical aversion of troop-contributing countries to sending their men into combat where they risk heavy casualties will act as a serious constraint on UN action in such areas for the foreseeable future. The development of UN forces that look more like SWAT (Special Weapons and Tactics) teams than conventional peacekeeping forces may, in fact, be necessary, but it takes the UN well beyond the current peacekeeping regime into uncharted waters. Whether and how the UN should proceed needs to be carefully explored and thoughtfully planned. A U.S. role in helping to chart the course is essential.

First Loyalty

Often troop-contributing governments can help quell on-the-ground crises, particularly when effective diplomatic pressure is applied to one or more of the belligerents. But in some cases their role is counterproductive. Although soldiers serving under the UN flag are supposed to owe their first loyalty to the UN and to their peacekeeping mission, national governments are often jealous of their prerogatives and are reluctant to adopt a hands-off attitude. In dangerous situations national contingents may coordinate their orders with their respective defense ministries before executing them. This means that precisely when a UN commander needs his soldiers to respond quickly, he may have to wait hours before his instructions are accepted; and sometimes the instructions are not accepted at all. There is no way to eliminate the penchant of governments to stay in touch with their soldiers. Yet it would be appropriate for the secretary-general to remind peacekeepers continually that they serve under his command and to indicate how national channels can endanger international effectiveness.

Peacekeepers are not intended to fight pitched battles or conduct extensive combat operations. When they use force, they do so in a measured, restrained way to quell violence, not to provoke further bloodshed. This restraint is essential if they are to maintain moral superiority in comparison to regular and irregular military forces. But the creative use of limited force or, even better, the innovative employment of military skills is by no means precluded. In 1974 a resourceful and courageous commander deployed troops of all his contingents at the Nicosia airport while the secretary-general exerted massive diplomatic pressure on Turkey. Together they deterred the Turkish forces from seizing a key parcel of Cypriot real estate.

What might have happened if the UN commander had been similarly resourceful in the early days of Israel's 1982 invasion of Lebanon? Without firing a shot at the formidable invasion force, the pace of the invasion could have been disrupted for some hours or even a few days had the UN force established a system of roadblocks and obstructions along the narrow roads and mountain passes of southern Lebanon. With the exception of a handful of Nepalese soldiers who bravely stood their ground on a bridge, UN contingents watched as the invaders passed through their lines. Consider the powerful imagery of Tiananmen Square where a single man stopped a tank column, and imagine the impact of a comparable picture showing the commander of an internationally recognized peacekeeping force refusing to permit a column of Israeli tanks to pass his headquarters. No such photograph exists.

If the invasion had been a complete surprise, the failure would have been easier to excuse. But the invasion had been anticipated for at least six months. Therefore, understandably, a few senior

By Jeff MacNelly for the *Chicago Tribune,* 1982.
Reprinted by permission: Tribune Media Services.

officials involved with the force remain deeply embarrassed about its performance. Had the UN force behaved with greater ingenuity and a deeper commitment to its mission, it would have won a moral victory of considerable proportions. It is even possible that if the Israeli forces had been delayed a day or two, the Israeli government would have been less inclined to pursue its mission in Lebanon.

Peacekeepers need to think about such situations before they happen, and this is one of the key responsibilities of the UN leadership. Thus, another merit of an effective military staff in New York would be to provide a structure that ensures that field commanders are planning ahead as peacekeepers are engaged in a growing number of dangerous situations. Superior military, in contrast to purely political, skills will be essential for future UN operations.

The Soviets have begun examining what the exact role of firepower in UN forces should be. The inherent limitations of moral as opposed to physical barriers raise questions about the credibility of peacekeepers. The early days of the Namibia operation aptly demonstrated the need for a greater military presence on the border where the UN was not effectively in a position to either interdict infiltrations by pro-independence rebels or halt South Africa's reprisals. For that matter, it was not even in a position to report independently.

In southern Lebanon there is a Force Mobile Reserve (FMR), a fleet of armored personnel carriers equipped with mortars and manned by soldiers from several countries. The FMR has sometimes successfully allowed the UN to "bare its teeth" and come to the rescue of peacekeepers. A similar type of arrangement may be necessary for the proposed peacekeeping force that has been agreed to in principle for Cambodia. If approved, it promises to be the largest and most dangerous operation since the Congo. This proposed force would not just need extraordinary mobility in very difficult terrain, but also the ability to crush likely outbreaks of violence in distant parts of the country. An FMR for Cambodia would need both armored personnel carriers and a squadron of armed helicopters. Even more important, to be successful such a force would have to be much more competent than UN forces have usually been in joint operations. It is doubtful that such a complex operation would succeed without considerable predeployment training and a mandate that is significantly different from those of previous UN operations.

Some of the nations most deeply committed to peacekeeping run large-scale training facilities to prepare their soldiers for UN duty. For example, Finland operates a first-rate center at Niinisalo where Finnish soldiers, as well as soldiers from several other countries, receive solid training. If peacekeeping is to meet its loftier expectations, facilities like those in Finland should be considered by other states and opened to many more officers and noncommissioned officers from developing countries.

4

Exploring New Frontiers

Though the rule is sometimes bent—as in Cyprus where the British, with their two sovereign base areas, have played a major role in peacekeeping since its inception, and in Lebanon where French paratroopers have occasionally been part of the UN presence—UN Security Council permanent members' forces are customarily excluded from UN operations. But the superpowers, both of whom provided key logistical help in launching operations in Namibia and along the Iran-Iraq border, could increase other forms of assistance, including training and perhaps intelligence-sharing, as well as support to the humanitarian side of peacekeeping operations.

Some experts favor using Soviet and American troops as reserves for UN forces. The presence of superpower troops on the ground would have a powerful symbolic and real impact on multilateral diplomacy, but whether that impact would actually enhance peacekeeping is an open question.

The supposition is that the inclusion of permanent members' forces would demonstrate firm international support and resolve, and that backup firepower by the superpowers would indicate serious commitment without continuous provocation on the ground. However, so many strings would probably be attached to great-power support as to make it irrelevant to most peacekeeping situations. For instance, any direct U.S. military support for the proposed UN operations in Cambodia would probably be severely circumscribed by public opinion in the United States, not to mention congressional restrictions.

As Moscow and Washington explore the boundaries of their evolving relationship, there is more than a little concern, especially in the Third World, about how the rest of the world will be affected. However implausible the possibility of a superpower "condominium," it is one that worries other nations. If the prospect of being caught in the middle of superpower competition is unattractive, the possibility of being the object of superpower cooperation can also be worrisome. As a Swahili folk proverb ruefully notes, the grass gets crushed whether the elephants are fighting or making love.

Problems of superpower involvement notwithstanding, the center of gravity of the peacekeeping discourse has begun to shift closer to enforcement actions and away from peacekeeping as practiced in the past. Though this development has been largely unnoticed outside of New York and some academic circles, the time may be approaching when the Security Council will, for the first time, actually direct a military enforcement action under Chapter VII of the Charter. In this context, Security Council Resolution 598 was the basis upon which the Persian Gulf war was brought to a close and was a watershed in cooperation among the permanent five. It was the first resolution ever to threaten sanctions in order to end a regional conflict between two independent states.

Options

In this climate of exploration, a number of options for enhancing the peacekeeping mechanism, and even moving beyond it, are being considered. Peacekeeping operations on the seas and in the air are one example. The initial enthusiasm of the Soviets for naval peacekeeping reflected their keen interest in displacing

U.S. and other Western naval forces from the Persian Gulf. Two former U.S. cabinet members, Cyrus Vance and Elliot Richardson, were convinced that a UN action would serve U.S. interests and be far less dangerous and costly than some 40 Western warships. While their proposal to place UN flags on merchant ships was not implemented, it launched an important debate. Now that the Persian Gulf war has ended, the international community has a stake in clearing the deadly debris of the conflict. A mine-clearing task force under the UN flag, financed by the oil-producing littoral nations and tanker owners, could provide a very useful demonstration of UN naval force in action.

There would also be major advantages to a UN aerial surveillance and airlift capacity, perhaps supplied and piloted jointly by staff from the air forces of the United States and the U.S.S.R. UN forces are, by design, deployed without any intelligence-gathering apparatus. Yet peacekeepers must maintain an accurate evaluation of the situation in their area of operations. Aerial surveillance is one way to provide crucial information. With it, force commanders could anticipate problems and verify compliance with a wide range of agreements. Data from the extensive and expensive intelligence-gathering network employed worldwide by the superpowers could be supplied routinely to the UN with only negligible additional costs. Moreover, if overflights of the 23 countries of NATO and the Warsaw Pact become routine after the signing of an "open-skies" agreement, similar aerial intelligence-gathering for peacekeeping operations would be a logical extension. Some Soviet and American equipment could be applied to UN tasks.

As technology improves and becomes generally available and acceptable, another promising area to be explored would be verification and monitoring. There are sound reasons to apply the lessons of objective UN monitoring, conducted so successfully by peacekeepers in the past, to a variety of new situations.

First, the use of high technology under UN control—from sensors to satellites—could save substantially in manpower expenditures. These are the bulk of the UN's present peacekeeping costs and hence deficits.

Second, objective outside verification is a requisite element of most agreements—from arms control to elections—to mitigate regional conflicts. Monitoring and verification are, for example, the key in proposals to end the 20-year war in Cambodia. The UN's involvement in Central America merits careful scrutiny as a precedent on both scores. This experience could be directly applicable to many other Third World hot spots—for instance, Afghanistan, Ethiopia, Angola, Mozambique, the Sudan—where lasting peace will require disarming heavily armed dissidents and supervising the conduct of elections to make certain they are genuinely representative.

Moscow's proposals for preventive diplomacy—stationing armed troops or observers from UN reserves on the border of any state that asks for them—are intriguing but flawed on several counts. Placing troops on one side of a border could lead peacekeepers to be drawn into battle if the hostile neighbor attacks. By playing the role of a firebreak, UN troops could become, from the point of view of the attacking country, part of the problem. Instead of preventing conflict, they could attract violence aimed at all defensive forces on the enemy's side of the border.

Special Case of Ministates

There is one problem area that might justify the UN's acquiring a more powerful military instrument. Small countries of minor geostrategic importance require outside assistance for their self-defense if they are to be viable and not spend a disproportionate share of the national budget on arms. A UN alternative to a U.S. intervention in Grenada or an Indian one in the Maldives, or even a French one in Chad or Zaïre, is feasible and might be desirable. In ministates, international forces, while running relatively low risks, would add immeasurably to national stability and security. The guarantee to small countries could perhaps become a first building block in an alternative security regime for ministates. As both the Palme Commission and the Commonwealth Expert Group on Small States recognize, small countries could turn to an international force for self-defense, using reductions in their military expenditures to pay the bill.

Talking It Over

A Note for Students and Discussion Groups

This issue of the HEADLINE SERIES, like its predecessors, is published for every serious reader, specialized or not, who takes an interest in the subject. Many of our readers will be in classrooms, seminars or community discussion groups. Particularly with them in mind, we present below some discussion questions—suggested as a starting point only—and references for further reading.

Discussion Questions

What are the principal tenets of peacekeeping? What is the difference between peacekeeping and peacemaking? What is "collective security" and why has it not been used? Why is peacekeeping described as Chapter Six and a Half of the UN Charter? Have all peacekeeping operations occurred under UN auspices?

Why was the Soviet Union so skeptical about UN peacekeeping for almost the first four decades of the organization's existence? What happened to change its negative attitude? When?

When and why did the United States change from the champion of multilateralism in Third World conflicts to the leading debtor? What can be done?

Why has financing become such a constraint on the UN's operations? What can be done about the financial crisis of peacekeeping? What are some of the present management problems? Based on U.S. experience with the waste inherent in a massive military budget, is it possible to design a watchdog agency that would ensure that peacekeeping budgets are spent wisely? What is the comparative cost of international intervention in relation to national defense expenditures? Is peacekeeping a solution in itself or must diplomacy be applied simultaneously?

Have UN peacekeepers been more effective in international or intranational conflicts? What role does (and should) the use of force play in peacekeeping?

How and where should UN peacekeepers be used in the future?

READING LIST

Alan, James, *Peacekeeping in International Politics*. London, Macmillan, 1990.

Diehl, Paul F., "Peacekeeping Operations and the Quest for Peace." *Political Science Quarterly,* Spring 1988.

Erskine, Lt. Gen. Emmanuel A., *Mission with Unifil: An African Soldier's Reflections*. London, Hurst, 1989.

Katz, Mark, *Gorbachev's Military Policy in the Third World*. New York, Praeger, 1989.

Luck, Edward C., and Gati, Toby Trister, "Gorbachev, the United Nations, and U.S. Policy." *The Washington Quarterly,* Fall 1988.

Mackinlay, John, *The Peacekeepers: An Assessment of Peacekeeping Operations at the Arab-Israeli Interface*. London, Unwin Hyman, 1989. A good discussion of the differences between UN and non-UN forces.

McDermott, Anthony, and Skjelsbaek, Kjell, eds., *The Multinational Force in Lebanon*. Gainesville, University Presses of Florida, 1991.

Nelson, Richard W., "Multinational Peacekeeping in the Middle East and the United Nations Model." *International Affairs,* Winter 1984–85.

Rikhye, Indar Jit, *The Theory and Practice of Peacekeeping*. London, Hurst, 1984.

Rubinstein, Robert A., "Cultural Analysis and International Security." *Alternatives,* Vol. 13, 1988. Excellent critique of the rational model so favored by power realists, and, at the same time, a good case for anthropological perspectives on security problems.

Survival, May/June 1990. A special issue devoted to peacekeeping, published by the International Institute for Strategic Studies.

Thant, U, *View from the UN.* London, David & Charles, 1977.

Urquhart, Brian E., *A Life in Peace and War.* New York, Harper and Row, 1987. An eloquent and informed account of a number of episodes of UN peacekeeping operations by one of its most widely respected diplomatic practitioners.

————, "The United Nations System and the Future." *International Affairs,* Spring 1989.

Weiss, Thomas G., ed., *The United Nations and Conflict Management: American, Soviet and Third World Views.* New York, International Peace Academy, 1990. The International Peace Academy has begun publishing *Occasional Papers* on such topical peacekeeping and peacemaking themes as financing and management.

————, and Kessler, Meryl A., "Moscow's U.N. Policy." *Foreign Policy,* Summer 1990. Authors state that "the Kremlin has become perhaps the most active and vocal advocate for a more dynamic UN."

Wiseman, Henry, ed., *Peacekeeping: Appraisals and Proposals.* New York, Pergamon Press, 1983.

Chronology of Current UN Peacekeeping Operations, Including Mandates and Troop Contributors

(beginning with the most recent)

Onuca (UN Observer Group in Central America) 1989–present

- To conduct on-site verification of the cessation of aid to irregular forces and the nonuse of the territory of one country for attacks on other countries, as well as to disarm Nicaraguan insurgents.

- 4 contributors to date: Canada, Colombia, Spain and Venezuela.

Untag (UN Transition Assistance Group) 1989–present

- To ensure free and fair elections for the Namibian people.

- 22 contributors to date: Australia, Bangladesh, Britain, Canada, Czechoslovakia, Denmark, Finland, Federal Republic of Germany, India, Ireland, Italy, Kenya, Malaysia, Panama, Pakistan, Peru, Poland, Spain, Sudan, Switzerland, Togo and Yugoslavia.

Unavem (UN Angola Verification Mission) 1989–present

- To monitor the withdrawal of Cuban troops from Angola.

- 10 contributors to date: Algeria, Argentina, Brazil, Congo, Czechoslovakia, India, Jordan, Norway, Spain and Yugoslavia.

Uniimog (UN Iran-Iraq Military Observer Group) 1988–present

- To observe cease-fire, monitor troop withdrawals, and assist in the exchange of war prisoners.

- 26 contributors to date: Argentina, Australia, Austria, Bangladesh, Canada, Denmark, Finland, Ghana, Hungary, India, Indonesia, Ireland, Italy, Kenya, Malaysia, New Zealand, Nigeria, Norway, Peru, Poland, Senegal, Sweden, Turkey, Uruguay, Yugoslavia and Zambia.

Ungomap (UN Good Offices Mission in Afghanistan and Pakistan) 1988–present

- To monitor Soviet troop withdrawal from Afghanistan.

- 10 contributors to date: Austria, Canada, Denmark, Fiji, Finland, Ghana, Ireland, Nepal, Poland and Sweden.

Unifil (UN Interim Force in Lebanon) 1978–present

- To confirm the withdrawal of Israeli forces from southern Lebanon, restore international peace and security, and assist the government of Lebanon in returning to effective control of the area.
- 14 contributors to date: Fiji, Finland, France, Ghana, Iran, Ireland, Italy, Nepal, Netherlands, Nigeria, Norway, Senegal, Sweden and the United States.

Undof (UN Disengagement Observer Force) 1974–present

- To supervise the cease-fire between Israel and Syria and establish a buffer zone.
- 9 contributors to date: Australia, Austria, Britain, Canada, Denmark, Finland, Ireland, New Zealand and Sweden.

Unficyp (UN Force in Cyprus) 1964–present

- To prevent the recurrence of fighting in Cyprus.
- 9 contributors to date: Australia, Austria, Britain, Canada, Denmark, Finland, Ireland, New Zealand and Sweden.

Unmogip (UN Military Observer Group in India and Pakistan)
1949–present

- To supervise the cease-fire between India and Pakistan in the State of Jammu and Kashmir.
- 10 contributors to date: Australia, Belgium, Canada, Chile, Denmark, Finland, Italy, New Zealand, Sweden and Uruguay.

Untso (UN Truce Supervision Organization) 1948–present

- Originally to supervise the cease-fire after the 1948 Arab-Israeli war, its mandate was extended and it currently deploys observers on the Golan Heights, in the Sinai and in southern Lebanon. The headquarters are in Jerusalem, but there are offices in Beirut, Amman, Damascus and Cairo.
- 18 contributors to date: Argentina, Australia, Austria, Belgium, Burma (Myanmar), Canada, Chile, Denmark, Finland, France, Ireland, Italy, Netherlands, New Zealand, Norway, Sweden, the U.S.S.R. and the United States.

From the Charter of the United Nations

CHAPTER IV

THE GENERAL ASSEMBLY

Article 19

A Member of the United Nations which is in arrears in the payment of its financial contributions to the Organization shall have no vote in the General Assembly if the amount of its arrears equals or exceeds the amount of the contributions due from it for the preceding two full years. The General Assembly may, nevertheless, permit such a Member to vote if it is satisfied that the failure to pay is due to conditions beyond the control of the Member.

CHAPTER VI

PACIFIC SETTLEMENT OF DISPUTES

Article 33

1. The parties to any dispute, the continuance of which is likely to endanger the maintenance of international peace and security, shall, first of all, seek a solution by negotiation, enquiry, mediation, conciliation, arbitration, judicial settlement, resort to regional agencies or arrangements, or other peaceful means of their own choice.

2. The Security Council shall, when it deems necessary, call upon the parties to settle their dispute by such means.

Article 34

The Security Council may investigate any dispute, or any situation which might lead to international friction or give rise to a dispute, in order to determine whether the continuance of the dispute or situation is likely to endanger the maintenance of international peace and security.

Article 35

1. Any Member of the United Nations may bring any dispute, or any situation of the nature referred to in Article 34, to the attention of the Security Council or of the General Assembly.

2. A state which is not a Member of the United Nations may bring to the attention of the Security Council or of the General Assembly any dispute to which it is a party if it accepts in advance, for the purposes of the dispute, the obligations of pacific settlement provided in the present Charter.

3. The proceedings of the General Assembly in respect of matters brought to its attention under this Article will be subject to the provisions of Articles 11 and 12.

Article 36

1. The Security Council may, at any stage of a dispute of the nature referred to in Article 33 or of a situation of like nature, recommend appropriate procedures or methods of adjustment.

2. The Security Council should take into consideration any procedures for the settlement of the dispute which have already been adopted by the parties.

3. In making recommendations under this Article the Security Council should also take into consideration that legal disputes should as a general rule be referred by the parties to the International Court of Justice in accordance with the provisions of the Statute of the Court.

Article 37

1. Should the parties to a dispute of the nature referred to in Article 33 fail to settle it by the means indicated in that Article, they shall refer it to the Security Council.

2. If the Security Council deems that the continuance of the dispute is in fact likely to endanger the maintenance of international peace and security, it shall decide whether to take action under Article 36 or to recommend such terms of settlement as it may consider appropriate.

Article 38

Without prejudice to the provisions of Articles 33 to 37, the Security Council may, if all the parties to any disputes so request, make recommendations to the parties with a view to a pacific settlement of the dispute.

CHAPTER VII

ACTION WITH RESPECT TO THREATS TO THE PEACE, BREACHES OF THE PEACE, AND ACTS OF AGGRESSION

Article 39

The Security Council shall determine the existence of any threat to the peace, breach of the peace, or act of aggression and shall make recommendations, or decide what measures shall be taken in accordance with Articles 41 and 42, to maintain or restore international peace and security.

Article 40

In order to prevent an aggravation of the situation, the Security Council may, before making the recommendations or deciding upon the measures provided for in Article 39, call upon the parties concerned to comply with such provisional measures as it deems necessary or desirable. Such provisional measures shall be without prejudice to the rights, claims, or position of the parties concerned. The Security Council shall duly take account of failure to comply with such provisional measures.

Article 41

The Security Council may decide what measures not involving the use of armed force are to be employed to give effect to its decisions, and it may call upon the Members of the United Nations to apply such measures. These may include complete or partial interruption of economic relations and of rail, sea, air, postal, telegraphic, radio, and other means of communication, and the severance of diplomatic relations.

Article 42

Should the Security Council consider that measures provided for in Article 41 would be inadequate or have proved to be inadequate, it may take such action by air, sea, or land forces as may be necessary to maintain or restore international peace and security. Such action may include demonstrations, blockade, and other operations by air, sea, or land forces of Members of the United Nations.

Article 43

1. All Members of the United Nations, in order to contribute to the maintenance of international peace and security, undertake to make available to the Security Council, on its call and in accordance with a special agreement or agreements, armed forces, assistance, and facilities, including rights of passage, necessary for the purpose of maintaining international peace and security.

2. Such agreement or agreements shall govern the numbers and types of forces, their degree of readiness and general location, and the nature of the facilities and assistance to be provided.

3. The agreement or agreements shall be negotiated as soon as possible on the initiative of the Security Council. They shall be concluded between the Security Council and Members or between the Security Council and groups of Members and shall be subject to ratification by the signatory states in accordance with their respective constitutional processes.

Article 44

When the Security Council has decided to use force it shall, before calling upon a Member not represented on it to provide armed forces in fulfilment of the obligations assumed under Article 43, invite that Member, if the Member so desires, to participate in the decisions of the Security Council concerning the employment of contingents of that Member's armed forces.

Article 45

In order to enable the United Nations to take urgent military measures, Members shall hold immediately available national air-force contingents for combined international enforcement action. The strength and degree of readiness of these contingents and plans for their combined action shall be determined, within the limits laid down in the special agreement or agreements referred to an Article 43, by the Security Council with the assistance of the Military Staff Committee.

Article 46

Plans for the application of armed force shall be made by the Security Council with the assistance of the Military Staff Committee.

Article 47

1. There shall be established a Military Staff Committee to advise and assist the Security Council on all questions relating to the Security Council's military requirements for the maintenance of international peace and security, the employment and command of forces placed at its disposal, the regulation of armaments, and possible disarmament.

2. The Military Staff Committee shall consist of the Chiefs of Staff of the permanent members of the Security Council or their representatives. Any Member of the United Nations not permanently represented on the Committee shall be invited by the Committee to be associated with it when the efficient discharge of the Committee's responsibilities requires the participation of that Member in its work.

3. The Military Staff Committee shall be responsible under the Security Council for the strategic direction of any armed forces placed at the disposal of the Security Council. Questions relating to the command of such forces shall be worked out subsequently.

4. The Military Staff Committee, with the authorization of the Security Council and after consultation with appropriate regional agencies, may establish regional subcommittees.

Article 48

1. The action required to carry out the decisions of the Security Council for the maintenance of international peace and security shall be taken by all the Members of the United Nations or by some of them, as the Security Council may determine.

2. Such decisions shall be carried out by the Members of the United Nations directly and through their action in the appropriate international agencies of which they are members.

Article 49

The Members of the United Nations shall join in affording mutual assistance in carrying out the measures decided upon by the Security Council.

Article 50

If preventive or enforcement measures against any state are taken by the Security Council, any other state, whether a Member of the United Nations or not, which finds itself confronted with special economic problems arising from the carrying out of those measures shall have the right to consult the Security Council with regard to a solution of those problems.

Article 51

Nothing in the present Charter shall impair the inherent right of individual or collective self-defence if an armed attack occurs against a Member of the United Nations, until the Security Council has taken measures necessary to maintain international peace and security. Measures taken by Members in the exercise of this right of self-defence shall be immediately reported to the Security Council and shall not in any way affect the authority and responsibility of the Security Council under the present Charter to take at any time such action as it deems necessary in order to maintain or restore international peace and security.

Draft Formulae for Articles
of
Agreed Guidelines for UN Operations

Title

Draft articles of guidelines for future United Nations peace-keeping operations under the authority of the Security Council and in accordance with the Charter of the United Nations.

Introduction

The aim of the present draft guidelines is to ensure, by the acceptance of principles and the institution of methods, that peace-keeping operations shall be used in the common interests of the United Nations.

Article 1

[(1) The Security Council has the authority over the establishment, direction and control of peace-keeping operations.]

(2) Responsibilities to be exercised directly by the Council in this respect are as follows:

1. Authorization;
2. Definition of purpose and mandate;
3. Kind of advice and assistance required by the Council;
4. Duration and related questions;
5. Financial arrangements;
6. Size (magnitude);
7. Authorization for appointment of deputy commanders;
8. Ultimate direction and control during the operation;
9. Subsequent alterations;
10. Agreements with contributing countries (model agreement and changes thereto);
11. Agreements with host-country (including model status of forces agreement and changes thereto);
12. Approval of roster of potential commanders.

Article 2

The Security Council may, in accordance with the provisions of the Charter of the United Nations, decide to delegate its authority over aspects of peace-keeping operations.

Article 3

In matters of peace-keeping all authority shall be exercised in conformity with relevant decisions of the Security Council.

Article 4

(1) The Security Council may, at the time of establishment of a peace-keeping operation, decide to establish a committee under Article 29 of the Charter in order to assist the Council in the performance of its functions. The committee shall be directly responsible to the Security Council.

(2) The committee shall consist of the following:

(a) The representatives of the five permanent members of the Security Council.

(b) The representatives of five non-permanent members designated by the Security Council, following a suitable system of rotation.

(c) The representatives of not more than five States designated by the Security Council from among those providing military contingents or personnel, also following a suitable system of rotation.

In the composition of the committee equitable geographical balance shall be one of the guiding principles.

(3) As a general rule, and unless the committee decides otherwise, the representatives of countries where the peace-keeping operation is being conducted may attend the meetings of the committee and participate in the discussions.

(4) Representatives of countries providing voluntarily on a substantial scale financial and other material contributions such as facilities, service and equipment may be invited to attend the metings of the committee and participate in the discussions.

(5) The Secretary-General or his representative shall attend the meetings of the committee.

(6) The committee shall meet as frequently as necessary for its work. It may also be convened at any time at the request of any one of its members, the Secretary-General, or the representative of a country where a peace-keeping operation is being conducted.

(7) The committee shall report to the Security Council at its request. In addition, the committee may make special reports, with recommendations, if any, on matters regarding the peace-keeping operation requiring decision or the attention of the Council.

(8) Decisions of the committee on procedural matters shall be made by an affirmative vote of a majority of the members of the committee. There will be no voting on other issues, and, in the absence of unanimity, the views expressed in the committee shall be reflected in the reports to the Security Council.

Article 5

The Security Council may delegate responsibilities to, or seek advice and assistance from, the Military Staff Committee established in accordance with Article 47 of the Charter of the United Nations. The Committee may invite any members of the United Nations, in particular any non-permanent members of the Security Council or any States providing contingents or facilities to associate themselves with it, when the efficient discharge of the Committee's responsibilities requires their participation in its work.

Article 6

The Secretary-General, under the authority of the Security Council, [shall direct the implementation of peace-keeping operations] [shall direct peace-keeping operations] [is in charge of the implementation of peace-keeping operations, receiving guidance from a subsidiary body of the Security Council] within the mandate entrusted to him by the

United Nations Charter, contributing with all means at his disposal to giving effect to relevant decisions of the Security Council.

Article 7

The Security Council shall receive reports, and may request special reports from, issue instructions to and receive recommendations from the Secretary-General and any subsidiary body which may be established.

Article 8

The command in the field will be exercised by a force commander appointment [on the proposal of the Secretary-General] [by the Secretary-General] [with the consent of] [by] the Security Council. The Commander will be given necessary authority over all elements of the operation within the terms of the mandate and specific directives. The Commander shall co-operate [through appropriate channels] with the subsidiary body which the Security Council may establish to assist the Council.

Article 9

It is essential that throughout the conduct of a United Nations peace-keeping operation it shall have the full confidence and backing of the Security Council. Such forces must operate with the full co-operation of the parties concerned, particularly of the Government of the host-country, due account being taken of its sovereignty. Such forces must function as integrated and efficient military units and act with complete objectivity. It is also of the utmost importance to secure freedom of movement for each unit irrespective of its nationality.

Article 10

In the composition of a peace-keeping force established under the authority of the Security Council equitable geographical balance shall be one of the guiding principles [along with the necessity of securing the over-all efficiency of the force]. [The selection and replacement of the national contingents shall be (undertaken) by the (Secretary-General with the) agreement of the Security Council and the host country.]

Article 11

The costs of peace-keeping operations authorized by the Security Council shall be considered as expenses of the Organization, to be borne by the members in accordance with Article 17, paragraph 2, of the Charter of the United Nations [or any other methods of financing which the Security Council may decide] [unless decided otherwise].

Article 12

[To ensure the state of readiness of the United Nations for prompt and effective establishment of peace-keeping operations, the Security Council may take steps to facilitate the conclusion of agreements, whether for forces, assistance, or facilities under Article 43 or other preparedness arrangements, in order fully to develop its peace-keeping capacity.] Such [agreements] [arrangements] may provide that specific contingents can be employed by the Council in a particular operation with the consent of the respective Governments.

Article 13

To ensure the effective functioning of the operation, United Nations forces will enjoy privileges and immunities in accordance with legal arrangements on the status of forces to be decided by agreement between the United Nations and the host-country.

Abbreviations in Text

Asean	Association of Southeast Asian Nations
CMF	Commonwealth Monitoring Fund
FMR	Force Mobile Reserve
IDF	Israeli Defense Forces
MFO	Multinational Force and Observers
MNF	Multinational Force in Beirut
MSC	Military Staff Committee
OAS	Organization of American States
OAU	Organization of African Unity
ONUC	UN Operation in the Congo
ORCI	Office of Research and Collection of Information
PLO	Palestine Liberation Organization
SWAT	Special Weapons and Tactics
Undof	UN Disengagement Observer Force
Unesco	UN Educational, Scientific and Cultural Organization
Unficyp	UN Force in Cyprus
Unicef	UN Children's Fund
Unifil	UN Interim Force in Lebanon
Untag	UN Transition Assistance Group
Untso	UN Truce Supervision Organization